Dinosaurs Kids Book

Billy Grinslott

Kinsey Marie Books

ISBN 9781957881874

Often compared to an army tank, Ankylosaurus had a heavily armored shell with a large club-like protrusion at the end of its tail. Ankylosaurus means fused lizard, and it was given that name because bones in its skull and other parts of its body were fused, making the dinosaur extremely rugged with a hard shell. Ankylosaurus clubbed tail could shatter other dinosaur's bones. Ankylosaurus was a plant-eating dinosaur that was the largest of its family of dinosaurs called ankylosaurs.

Allosaurus. You pronounce their name 'al-low-sauw-us'. Their length was around 28 feet. They weighed about 4 tons. Allosaurus was constantly shedding and regrowing new teeth. They had a large head and used their big tail to balance themselves. The backbone of this dinosaur was different to that of other dinosaurs, which is where the meaning of the name different lizard comes from. They were not as big as some dinosaur's, but for their size they were very ferocious and were feared by other dinosaur's. Allosaurus was one of the first dinosaur movie stars.

Archaeopteryx, this animal had a coat of feathers, a bird-like beak, a handful of teeth, a long, bony tail, and three claws on each of its wings. Which are all reptilian characteristics that are not seen in any modern birds. For these reasons, it's every bit as accurate to call Archaeopteryx a dinosaur as it is to call it a bird. Many people believe this dino-bird was much larger than it actually was. In fact, Archaeopteryx measured only about 20 inches from head to tail, about the size of a well-fed, modern-day pigeon.

The Baryonyx had oversized claws on Its thumbs and was a close relative of Spinosaurus. It's favorite food was fish. It's jaws were angled to keep prey from wriggling free. It had twice as many teeth as the T-Rex. The snout of the Baryonyx was unlike that of most dinosaurs. It was long and narrow, with rows of, finely serrated teeth. The serrated teeth are just like crocodiles. The Baryonyx was a medium-sized dinosaur that walked on two legs. Although it wasn't fully aquatic, it spent a lot of time in or near water. It had many adaptations to water, which were likely to have been used to catch fish.

The Brachiosaurus had a long neck. It also had longer front legs than hind legs. They used their long necks to eat leaves off of trees. Their length was around 85 feet. They weighed about 40 tons. Brachiosaurus is considered to be the largest dinosaur's known. They stood 30 feet tall at the hips.

The Brontosaurs also had a long neck for eating trees and other plants. They weighed about 17 tons and were about 72 feet long. Estimates put the weight of a Brontosaurus up to 17 tons. Paleontologists believe the Brontosaurus had a lifespan up to 100 years. The nostrils of a Brontosaurus were located on the top of its head. It takes about 10 years for them to grow to full size. They could walk on land and in the water.

Carcharodontosaurus was a huge dinosaur. This dinosaur had a massive tail, a bulky body, and big heavy bones. Its arms were short and had three-fingered hands with sharp claws. Although the Carcharodontosaurus was larger than a T-Rex, its brain was smaller. Carcharodontosaurus is believed to have been a fearsome dinosaur. It was about 44 feet long and could weigh as much as 7 ½ tons.

The Carnotaurus is one of the fastest theropods to ever live on our planet. They had a top speed of up to 35 miles per hour. To date the Carnotaurus is the only dinosaur known to have possessed horns, six inches long on top of its eyes. The name Carnotaurus means meat eating bull. They could grow up to 28 feet in length and weigh up to 2,200 pounds. The teeth of a Carnotaurus are about eight times smaller than teeth of a Tyrannosaurus Rex.

Ceratosaurus. You pronounce their name sih-rat-uh-saw-rus. Its name means Horned Lizard. Their length was up to 20 feet. They weighed about 2200 pounds the size of a small car. Ceratosaurus was a medium sized dinosaur despite its strong build Ceratosaurus were quite likely nimble and able run to speeds of 20-30mph. Ceratosaurs had a deep tail and a flexible body. This would make it a good swimmer. It was 20 feet long and 13 feet high.

The Centrosaurus weighed about 2400 poumds. The Centrosaurus had a large parrot-like beak that was toothless and had a hard covering which helped this dinosaur to graze on plants. Their teeth were made for grinding and chewing hard plant materials. They had a ball and socket-type joint, which allowed them a free neck movement of their huge head. The skull length was longer than the frill length and the frill could attain a maximum length of 19 inches. They had strong legs, and their feet were hooflike claws. The tail was very light weighted and short and did not touch the ground.

The Dilophosaurus was a medium-sized dinosaur and one of the first large predatory dinosaurs. The Dilophosaurus was 20 feet long and weighed around 1,000 pounds. The Dilophosaurus is has paired crests on top of its skull. They were stealthy and light on their feet. The Dilophosaurus does not spit venom like some movies portray.

The Deinonychus weighed up to 175 pounds, and it was about five feet tall and ten feet long. The Deinonychus was a fast runner who probably traveled in packs. This dinosaur could run at speeds up to 25 miles per hour. The Deinonychus was also one of the most intelligent dinosaurs, which spelled trouble for other dinosaurs because it could outwit and out think them. It had three claws on its hands and a large talon on the back legs. They say that some species had feathers, but it may or may not be true.

Diplodocus are the longest known dinosaur. Their length was up to 88 feet. They weighed about 12 tons, as much as a large truck. Diplodocus front legs were shorter than its hind legs. The neck and tail of Diplodocus consisted of almost 100 vertebrae. Diplodocus were herbivorous, meaning they only ate plants. Its narrow teeth were arranged like a rake, which helped them strip leaves from gingko and conifer trees. They had very tiny brains compared to how big they were. A full grown Diplodocus had no natural enemies because of its size.

The Dryptosaurus was a large, bipedal, meaning it walked on two feet. It was a ground-dwelling dinosaur, that grew up to 25 feet long and weighed up to 3.300 pounds. This dinosaur could run at speeds up to 25 miles per hour. Each of its 3 fingers were tipped by an eight-inch, talon-like claw, with razor sharp teeth. It was one of the only dinosaurs to have fur patches.

Part of what has made Giganotosaurus famous, is the fact that it outweighed the Tyrannosaurus Rex. Full-grown adults may have tipped the scales at about 12 tons, compared to a little over ten tons for a female T. Rex. Not only did it out weigh the T-Rex, it was faster. But it had one flaw compared to the T-Rex, its brain was much smaller, which gave it a disadvantage when facing a T-Rex. The Giganotosaurus and T-Rex grew to about the same length of 40 feet, but the Giganotosaurus out weighed the T-rex.

The Gorgosaurus was a finely balanced and had large, muscular and powerful legs, being more agile than Tyrannosaurus rex and likely able to reach a top speed of around 30 mph. The only difference was the size, they only grew to about 30 feet in length and weighed less. The Gorgosaurus was a member of the Tyrannosauridae family the same family as Tyrannosaurus Rex.

The Iguanodon was an herbivore which means it ate plants. Their length was up to 39 feet, and they weighed 3.5 tons. They were pretty slow compared to some dinosaurs and could only run about 15 mph. The Iguanodon had a really long little finger which it used to gather food. Their thumbs had spikes on top to help them grab food. Their teeth were designed to help them chew tough plants. It was one of the first dinosaurs to be publicly displayed.

The Megalosaurus was the first dinosaur ever to be named a dinosaur by scientists The Megalosaurus was only about half the length of Tyrannosaurus Rex, About 21 feet long and one-eighth of its weight. Making it small compared to some larger dinosaurs. It was agile for its size, but could only run about 20 mph. Making it slow compared to some other dinosaurs.

The Oviraptor is well known for being one of the most birdlike of all dinosaurs. This dinosaur possessed a sharp, toothless beak, and it sported a chicken-like wattle. The Oviraptor was almost certainly covered with feathers. The Oviraptor was an attentive parent, caring for their offspring.

The dome shaped head of a Pachycephalosaurs is believed to have been used by males for ramming into other dinosaurs. Pachycephalosaurs had a skull that was 30 times thicker and stronger than a modern-day human skull. They grew to be about 16 feet long, with strong hind legs. They were slow and could only run about 15 mph. The Pachycephalosaurs had two arms with five-clawed fingers and two legs with three-clawed toes.

The pterodactyl was by far the scariest dinosaur that could fly. They had sharp claws on both their feet and wings, along with a long sharp beak and a mouth full of teeth. Pterodactyls were the largest flying animals that ever lived. Some pterodactyls had a wing span of 36 feet, that's a huge wing span. They could fly at a speeds of over 67 mph for a few minutes and then glide at cruising speeds of about 56 mph. That's fast, its about the same speed a car drives down the highway.

The Spinosaurus was longer and heavier than the Tyrannosaurus Rex. The Spinosaurus is the largest known carnivorous dinosaur. It had a skull 6 feet long, a body length of 46–59 feet, and an it weighed 13–22 tons. What makes Spinosaurus special are its unique adaptations which allowed the dinosaur to hunt underwater. Like crocodiles, Spinosaurus had a long narrow snout with nostrils mid-skull, perfect for submerging under water.

The Stenonychosaurus was a small dinosaur, up to 3 feet in height, 8 feet in length, and weighed about 110 pounds. There have been 73 different types found by paleontologists. The build of Stenonychosaurus supported a fast-running lifestyle, it was quick and agile. It had sickle like claws on its feet, which gave it good traction while running. It is sometimes listed as the most intelligent of dinosaurs.

The Stegosaurus length was about 30 feet long. They were 14 feet tall. They weighed 2 tons, about the weight of an average American car. Stegosaurus had small heads and brains, their brain was about the size of a ping pong ball. They were slow and could only run about 4 mph. The Stegosaurus was an armored dinosaur, with large bone plates along its neck, back and tail. Its main diet was plants, it had no teeth and a beak like mouth for pulling and eating plants.

Styracosaurus had one of the most distinctive skulls of any frilled dinosaur, including an extra-long frill studded with four to six horns, a single, two-foot-long horn protruding from its nose, and shorter horns sticking out from each of its cheeks. Styracosaurus was moderately sized only weighing about 3 tons. They traveled in herds. The build of Styracosaurus resembles that of a modern day rhinoceros.

Tarbosaurus is related to T-rex, there are some key differences. Tarbosaurus had a longer skull and had about 60 teeth. more teeth than T-rex. Though the Tarbosaurus was big, it weighed less than the T-Rex, which gave it a disadvantage. Still, the Tarbosaurus was one of the biggest carnivore dinosaurs.

The Therizinosaurus most likely had feathers and it had very large claws that could be used for digging. It had longer claws than most other dinosaurs. One disadvantage they had was bad eyesight, they couldn't see very well. They stood about 10 feet high, they were 33 feet long, and weighed about 5 tons. They could run about 17 mph. Other dinosaurs feared the Therizinosaurus because of their long claws.

The Apatosaurus was another tall plant eating dinosaur. They had peg-shaped teeth with sharp, chiseled tips for eating vegetation. In order to get blood flow all, the way up to their long necks and heads, they had the strongest heart of most dinosaurs. They used their long tails to smack the ground and make a loud noise to scare off other dinosaurs. They stood about 15 feet tall at the hips, weighed about 40 tons and could be 70 feet long.

Triceratops means three-horned-face. The triceratops head is one of the largest of any land animal discovered. Some triceratops may have had as many as 800 teeth. The horn on the end of its snout, was made from a soft protein called keratin, just like human fingernails. Triceratops had an enormous skull with a backward pointing frill or hood that was about 7 feet long. Their main diet was plants. One of the lesser known facts about the Triceratops is that they had birdlike beaks and could clip off hundreds of pounds of tough vegetation every day.

The Utahraptor is the largest raptor yet to be discovered. The claws on Utahraptor's hind feet were almost a foot long. They were discovered in Utah and that's how they got their name. It had short, stocky legs for jumping great heights. It also had 5-inch-long front claws, that it would use to grab onto things. The Utahraptor also had a long tail to act as a counterbalance while it runs and helped it to turn and maneuver faster.

The velociraptor for its small size was one of the most feared dinosaurs. They were quick and could move very swiftly and jump high. They could jump 10 feet straight up in the air, that's amazing. They usually traveled in groups, which meant other dinosaurs had to deal with more than one at a time. They had sharp claws and teeth. They only grew up to 100 pounds, about the size of a wolf. But for their small size, they could contend with most other dinosaurs, because they were very fast and agile.

Tyrannosaurus Rex, known as the T-Rex. The T-Rex was one of the biggest dinosaurs. They could sprint up to 20 mph. Their length was up to 40 feet. Females were bigger than males. The T-Rex is one of the most famous dinosaurs and was feared by most other dinosaurs. As you can see they have a big mouth with lots of huge teeth, that's scary. The largest T-Rex tooth found is 12 inches long. Their bite force was 3 times stronger than any other dinosaur. They had a brute size force, a loud roar, lots of huge teeth and no fear of other dinosaurs, which made them one of the most feared dinosaurs and king of dinosaur land. The End.

Author Page

Billy Grinslott

Kinsey Marie Books

ISBN 9781957881874

Copyright, All Rights Reserved.

www.ingramcontent.com/pod-product-compliance
Lightning Source LLC
Chambersburg PA
CBHW041538040426
42446CB00002B/140